SOUTHERN INDIANA

PICTURE BOOKS BY HARTLEY AND JEAN ALLEY

A Gentleman from Indiana Looks at Marblehead

Southern Indiana

SOUTHERN INDIANA

PHOTOGRAPHED BY HARTLEY ALLEY

with text
by Jean Alley

INDIANA UNIVERSITY PRESS / BLOOMINGTON

Copyright © 1965 by Hartley Alley

Library of Congress catalog card number 65-11797

Designed by Jean Alley

Printed in the United States of America by

Halliday Lithograph Corp.

SOUTHERN INDIANA is a complex combination of modern-day efficiency and rural Americana. There are still the deep forests of pioneer America, the buildings of almost two centuries, and the traditions of early riverboat days. But there is also modern industry, some of the most avant-garde architecture of the twentieth century, and the cultural atmosphere of one of America's biggest universities.

The southern part of Indiana was settled before the rest of the state. It still retains the flavor of the pioneer days. For the history buff who wants to step back in time, there are an infinite number and variety of steps to take. At Vincennes he can see where George Rogers Clark saved the whole Northwest for the young American colonies by capturing Fort Sackville from the British in 1779. Near Gentryville Abraham Lincoln spent his boyhood years in a pioneer cabin on Pigeon Creek. Here in Spencer County the Nancy Hanks Lincoln State Park and the Lincoln Boyhood National Memorial offer the visitor a glimpse of what Lincoln's boyhood in Indiana must have been like. Kin Hubbard's fictional backwoods philosopher, Abe Martin, was copied after real-life Brown County settlers, and backwoods Brown County hasn't changed much since then. One of the few Civil War battles to be fought in the North was waged at Corydon. Morgan's famous Confederate raiders crossed the Ohio River near Mauckport in July of 1863 and engaged in the battle of Corydon before sweeping on north and east—through Salem, Vernon, Versailles, and Sunman—with Federal cavalry in hot pursuit.

The rivers of southern Indiana were the early superhighways. The Ohio River, flowing all along Indiana's southern border, brought pioneers by flatboat and packet to settle in the wilderness. Indiana's Ohio River towns are monuments to the early riverboat days. Madison, which became a center of wealth and refinement during the nineteenth century while most of the Midwest was still a wilderness, contains many restored houses of architectural merit. Aurora and Alton each has a beautiful riverboat-inspired mansion. Madison, Vevay, New Albany, Tell City, Evansville, Newburgh, and Mount Vernon are among the proud river towns that were the first to be settled in Indiana.

The Wabash River was the roadway for even earlier travelers—the French *coureur de bois* from Canada who trapped furs, and the French missionaries sent out to convert the Indians.

Of course, settlers also came to Indiana by covered wagon. The Michigan Road, which started at Madison, was an important gateway to the Northwest. The Buffalo Trace was a natural roadbed carved out by the hoofs of great herds of buffalo that for centuries made yearly treks across southern Indiana. From the bluegrass region of Kentucky the buffalo thundered north to cross the Ohio near New Albany—then on past French Lick to Vincennes and across the Wabash River to the plains of Illinois. The Buffalo Trace was the roadway for countless numbers of covered wagons as pioneers ventured into the deep forests of southern Indiana.

The history of southern Indiana can be traced through its architecture—from the log cabins built by unskilled homesteaders, through the elegant Federalist period, to the elaborate Gothic, and finally to the most advanced designs of today. Brown County still has hundreds of log cabins. The city of Columbus, just one county away, contains a score of outstanding examples of contemporary architecture designed by some of the world's most renowned architects.

This log cabin is in Spring Mill Village, a restored pioneer community that had its beginnings in 1814.

Here today's visitor can wander through the houses and shops of yesterday, visit the grist mill, and buy cornmeal that has been ground just as it was 150 years ago.

The steamboat Gothic windows (on page 9) are in New Albany, where once flourished a million-dollar-a-year industry in riverboat building. New Albany craftsmen turned out the steamboat *Robert E. Lee,* which was to become the most famous riverboat of all time when she won the New Orleans to St. Louis run in the historic race with the *Natchez* in 1870.

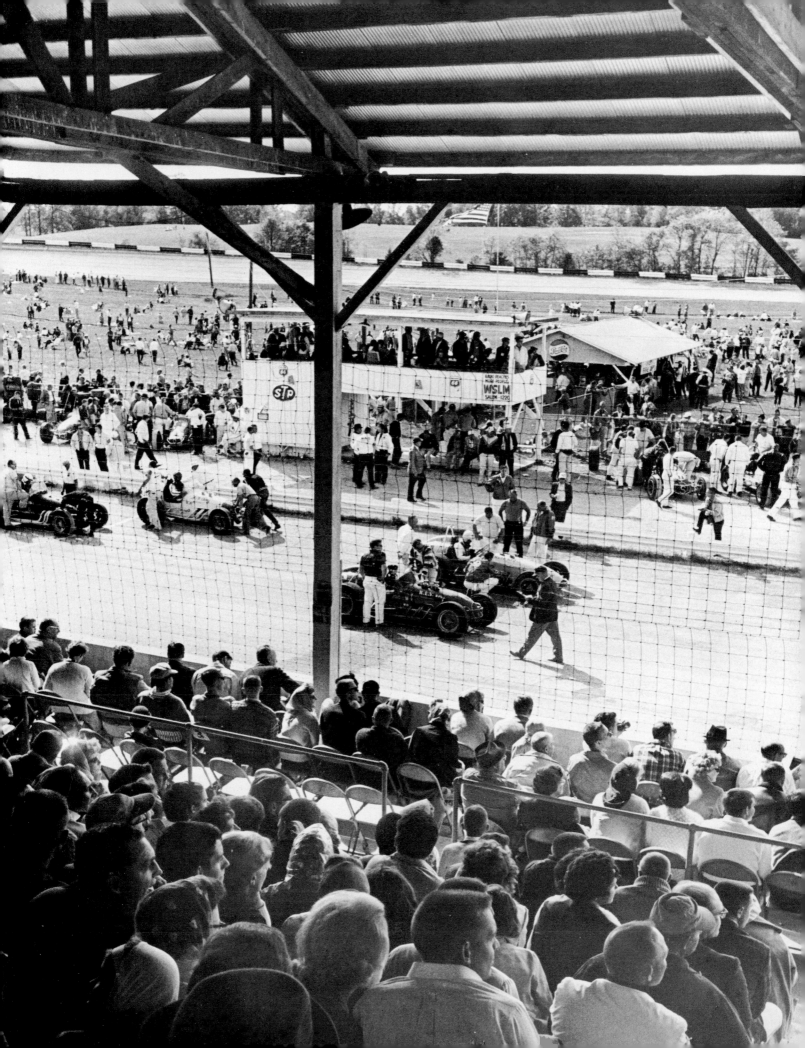

MADISON was founded in 1809 and became a center of culture in frontier America. It was a thriving river town—a gateway for settlers coming into the newly opened Indiana Territory, and logically the shipping point for products of the area which were to be sent out by riverboat.

Francis Costigan, perhaps Indiana's most noteworthy nineteenth-century architect, designed many of the houses in Madison, and there remains in Madison one of the largest collections of antebellum architecture in the country. Many of the delightful wrought-iron patterns to be found on Madison houses were designed by Francis Costigan and fabricated in Madison foundries. Other ornamental ironwork which was manufactured in Madison was shipped downriver by packet boat, some of it going as far as New Orleans where it was used in the old French Quarter.

The Shrewsbury House (at left) and the Lanier Mansion (on page 22) were both designed by Francis Costigan. They are excellent examples of early American architecture. The Jeremiah Sullivan house (below) was Madison's first mansion and is a beautiful example of Federal design. Built in 1818, it illustrates the breaking away from the English-inspired Georgian-Colonial toward a more truly American style of architecture.

VINCENNES stands on a spot that has been historically significant for hundreds of years. The Wabash River, furnishing the primary north-south route through the wilderness, and the Buffalo Trace, which was the important east-west roadway, crossed here. Indian tribes shared these hunting grounds before the coming of the white man—and in prehistoric times the Moundbuilders probably lived here.

In the seventeenth century French fur trappers and traders slid their canoes ashore at what is now Vincennes. They came to the Wabash from Quebec by way of the Great Lakes. The French established a fort at Vincennes, and this settlement became Indiana's first village. Parish records in the Old Cathedral (page 26) date from 1749, but it is probable that a Jesuit priest came to the wilderness as early as 1702.

After the French and Indian War the British controlled the area and built Fort Sackville. In 1779 George Rogers Clark and his small band of heroic Americans pushed through the icy February countryside from Fort Kaskaskia to capture Fort Sackville and secure the Northwest Territory for the United States.

Vincennes then became the first territorial capital, with William Henry Harrison as first governor of the Indiana and Louisiana Territories.

The George Rogers Clark Memorial (page 27) overlooking the Wabash River, stands on the site of Fort Sackville, commemorating the heroism of the early pioneers in the conquest of the West.

CORYDON, in Harrison County, was Indiana's first state capital. Here Indiana's early lawmakers met in a square rough-limestone building of exceptionally beautiful proportions and design. Today the building is restored and open to visitors. The state representatives met in the large first-floor room (facing page).

BROWN COUNTY is the heart of southern Indiana to many people. The rugged hill country has withstood the advances of modernization. Backwoods Brown County could be pioneer America give or take a few television antennas. Scattered throughout the hills are hundreds of log cabins—most of them lived in the year round. Tobacco and sorghum grow in little hillside plots, and every fall the natives turn out sorghum syrup by pressing the cane in horse-powered contraptions (page 33).

Nashville with a country store, art galleries, antique shops and a summer theater is a mecca for tourists from far and near.

Brown County is famous for its trees. Dogwood and redbud in the spring and flaming maple leaves in the fall are equally delightful.

Brown County has been an art colony since early in the century when T. C. Steele opened his studio in the woods near Nashville. C. Curry Bohm (left) is one of the deans of the colony, having painted here since 1932. A variety of art is available in Brown County, but the most popular kind seems to be sentimental scenic.

STONE HEAD

GNAW BONE

BEAN BLOSSOM

STONEY LONESOME

CONTEMPORARY DESIGN in architecture is also a part of southern Indiana. Perhaps the best examples are to be found in Columbus, a city of some 25,000 that is rumored to have more million- aires per capita than any other place in the country. A score of its new schools, homes, public buildings, and even a factory have been designed by some of the world's leading architects.

Small country churches are an integral part of the southern Indiana landscape. One comes to expect the white clapboard box-like structures that sit with dignity throughout the area. The North Christian Church in Columbus (right) sends its spire 135 feet skyward in a radical departure from the norm. It was designed by Eero Saarinen, his last project before his death, and a design that he considered one of his best.

INDIANA UNIVERSITY, founded in 1820 when Indiana was a young state, has become the eleventh largest university in the country. It is the educational and cultural center of not only southern Indiana, but indeed of the whole state of Indiana.

Indiana University boasts opera every Saturday night during the winter term, and in the summer a colossal under-the-stars production.

AGRICULTURE is southern Indiana's principal industry. Although there are great areas of hills and forests which are unsuitable for farming, there are also broad expanses of fertile land. In some counties huge fields of wheat or corn thrive under the hot Indiana sun. Legend has it that if you go into the middle of a cornfield on a hot summer night you can hear the corn grow with a whispered crackling that seems to come from nowhere and everywhere at once. Not many miles away you'll come to rocky hills that are completely unsuited for growing crops. Some of these lands have become cattle-raising areas —even look like Western ranches.

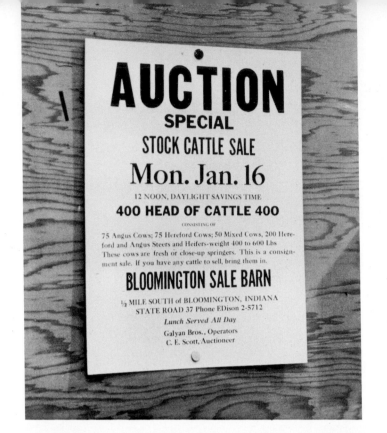

NEW HARMONY was the location of two early experiments in communal living. It was founded by the Rappites, a strict sect of German immigrants who were preparing themselves for the millennium. They lived a simple, celibate life in preparation for the expected end of the world.

Father George Rapp brought his followers to the Wabash Valley in 1814. They spent eleven years in Harmonie and created a prosperous, thriving community. Their houses were amazingly well-built and ingenious. They were insulated with a Rappite invention, "Dutch biscuits," made from slabs of wood wrapped in straw and mud and inserted in spaces between ceilings and floors. By some secret formula they managed to make their building materials termite-proof. On the walls of their homes were pegs where chairs and small tables could be hung up out of the way at housecleaning time.

The community prospered to such an extent that Father Rapp, fearing they were becoming too worldly, decided it was the Lord's will for them to leave Harmonie and start a new community else-where. Legend maintains that to persuade the Rappites to leave he told them the angel Gabriel had descended and spoken to him. Indeed to convince his followers he pointed to the angel's footprints in a slab of rock. Whether or not the legend is true, those footprints still exist in a stone slab in New Harmony.

The Rappites sold their town to Robert Owen, who aspired to establish a community of equality, where he expected universal knowledge to lead to universal happiness. Owen's "boatload of knowledge," which arrived in the wilderness by way of the Wabash River, was made up of brilliant men and women, but they lacked the practical skills to survive in pioneer America. The Owenite experiment was a failure, but during its two years in New Harmony it was responsible for many firsts, among them the first kindergarten in America, the first free public school for both boys and girls, the first trade school, the first civic dramatic club, and the first Workingmen's Institute and free library.

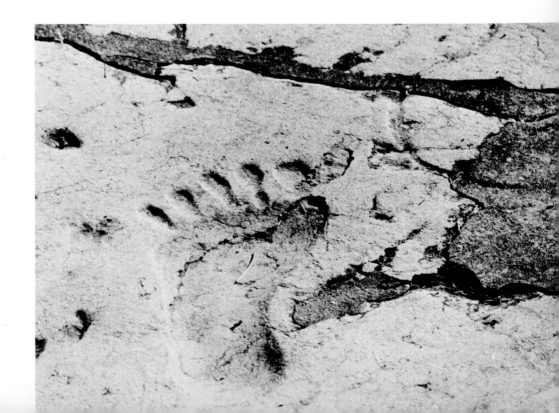

AUTHENTIC
Rappite Dwelling
Restored by
COLONIAL DAMES of AMERICA
FOR TOURS SEE
Mrs Watson - second house west towards river

The Owen Laboratory (left) was built by one of Robert Owen's sons, David Dale Owen. In 1839 he was appointed United States Geologist and New Harmony became the headquarters of the United States Geological Survey.

The Rose of Micah, symbol of the Rappites, was carved above their church door. Today that door is preserved in New Harmony's public school building. In startling visual contrast to the Rappite architecture, is the non-denominational shrine (above) called the Roofless Church.

Sat. Noon

Fried Chicken or
Ham – Choice of
Veg, Salads, Desserts
Cafeteria Style

at Catholic Center
By Methodist Church

Sat Nite

Beans
Sausage
Adults .6$1.00
Children $.50
Volunteer
Firemen
at Catholic Center

Methodist Church
Serving dinner
Sat. 11 – 1:30
Fried Chicken – Ham

Catholic Center – 419 Steam Mill

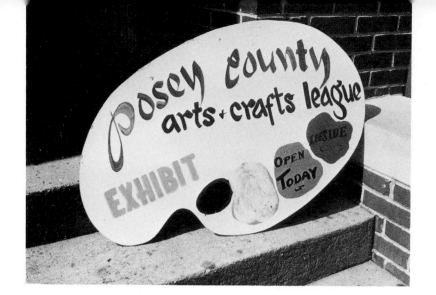

Picnicking is popular in southern Indiana at Spring Mill State Park or at any of the other parks scattered throughout the area. The stone mill (on page 69) in restored Spring Mill Village grinds cornmeal in the old-fashioned way—between great millstones driven by water power.

THE RIVERS of southern Indiana have always been important. In the early days they brought settlers to the newly opened frontier, and carried produce out to market. Today barges still navigate the rivers, loaded with coal and steel, sugar and grain.

The packets and showboats of the last century are gone, but any day you can see long lines of barges moving up and down the Ohio, pushed by sturdy diesel towboats. The *Delta Queen*, last of the passenger-carrying stern-wheelers, paddles its way from Cincinnati all along the southern edge of Indiana on its way to New Orleans. Indiana University's showboat provides old-time theatrical fare for summertime audiences. Houseboats, motor launches, hydroplanes, and sailboats continually ply the broad expanse of the rivers. The young Abe Lincoln once operated a ferryboat across the Ohio at Troy. Ferryboats still cross rivers at isolated spots where small Indiana towns need connections with small Kentucky and Illinois towns.

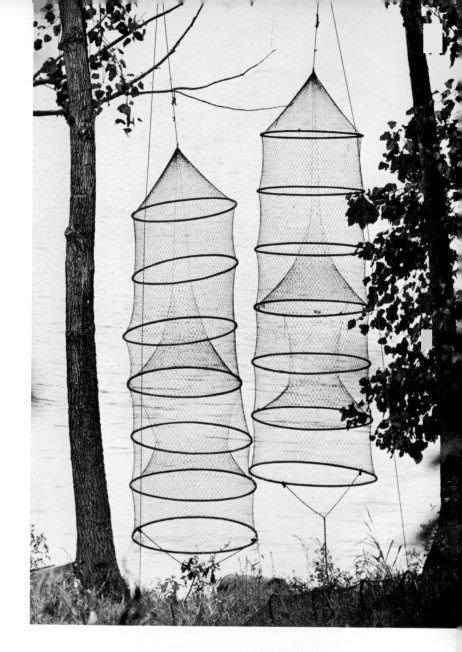

When Alton was a thriving river town, Steamboat Gothic was a favorite architectural style. A steamboat captain built this house in 1889 to remind him of his riverboat.

Hillforest in Aurora also looks like a riverboat, with the pilot house perched atop, and the graceful round lines of the porch echoing it. Both the exterior and the interior reflect the romantic steamboat era of the mid-nineteenth century in the Ohio Valley.

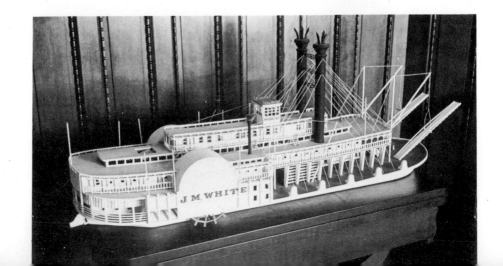

Wooden steamboats like the models on the facing page were once built in the Jeffersonville boatyards where today diesel-powered steel towboats and barges are turned out. These models are a part of the large collection in the Howard Steamboat Museum just across the street from the Jeff Boat Company.

The Indiana University Showboat brings old-time show business to Ohio river towns every summer. The calliope blares out over the river at twilight, and at night the showboat rides on the water with its lights sparkling like jewels.

BASKETBALL, the Hoosier Hysteria, is by far the most popular sport in southern Indiana.

THE WORLD IS NOT INTERESTED IN WHERE YOU HAVE BEEN, BUT WHERE YOU ARE GOING: NOT IN WHAT YOU HAVE DONE, BUT WHAT YOU ARE DOING.

Southern Indiana's lakes come in all sizes, from small ones like Starve Hollow Lake in Jackson County, to the largest in the state—the new Monroe Reservoir. The Monroe Reservoir covers 11,000 acres and its eighty-five miles of shoreline jut into three counties—Monroe, Brown, and Jackson.

FRENCH LICK AND WEST BADEN were famous spas in the days before Florida became fashionable. At the turn of the century these two hotels were dedicated to catering to the whims of the idle rich. The French Lick-Sheraton still carries on the traditions of resort vacationing. West Baden's hotel (below) is no longer in operation, but is worth a sightseeing tour. The tremendous, unsupported dome was called the eighth wonder of the world when it was built in 1901. For the weekend entertainment of guests, a complete circus would sometimes perform in the gigantic central court, and the dome would vibrate to the roars of lions, tigers, and elephants. Major league baseball clubs used to make West Baden their spring training headquarters. James J. Corbett trained here before the Corbett-Sharkey fight, and John L. Sullivan was a frequent visitor. Later on Al Capone was one of the West Baden guests, patrolling the grounds in his famous armored Lincoln. Gambling was a big attraction at these resorts, not only in the hotels but in numerous nearby casinos, and old-timers say that $50,000 bets were not unheard of.

During the season as many as twelve passenger trains a day pulled in and out of the depot. French Lick had a private railroad spur to bring guests like Diamond Jim Brady in their private railroad cars, practically to the front door. The original French Lick Hotel was built around the famous Pluto Water spring. It was the custom for guests to visit the Pluto spring each morning before breakfast, drink a cup of hot Pluto Water and take a morning constitutional along one of the many sawdust paths. Guests at the hotel today can still call the bell captain and order a cup of hot Pluto Water before breakfast.

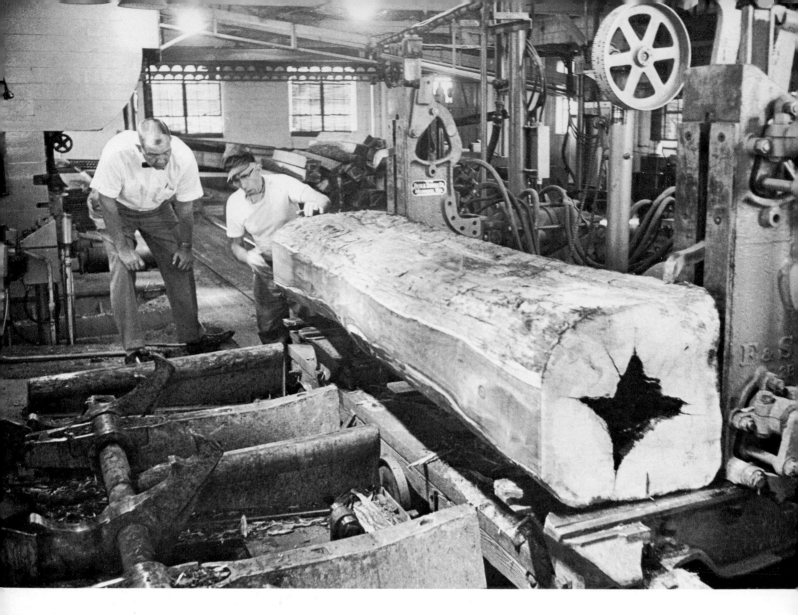

TRADITIONAL INDUSTRIES OF SOUTHERN INDI-
ANA include woodworking, stone quarrying, and
boatbuilding. A rosewood log from Brazil (above) is
being cut to make veneer in a New Albany factory.
Furniture making in Tell City (right) has been going
on for a hundred years. For longer than that, Hoosier
craftsmen like the axe-handle maker (pages 102 and
103) have worked with wood.

In the stone quarries scattered between Bedford
and Bloomington great blocks of limestone are hewn
out of the earth, piled up for seasoning, and then
carried away on trucks or trains (pages 10 through
109).

The delicate gold chair being inspected at the end of the assembly line in a Tell City chair factory is sometimes called the Jackie Kennedy chair. Four hundred and twenty-five of these chairs from Indiana are in the White House. Mrs. Kennedy selected them for use at White House receptions.

SENTIMENTALITY plays a big part in the Hoosier personality. The most typical Hoosier architecture may well be the ornate farmhouse, decorated lavishly with the carpenter's lace that was so popular in the nineteenth century.

Indianians are sentimentally attached to the name Hoosier. In Indiana the epithet denotes sincerity, affection, and a just-plain-folks friendliness. A cab driver in New York City might use the term in a derogatory sense, but a true Hoosier knows that there's nothing more flattering than to be called a Hoosier.

The origins of the name are obscure, but the most popular theory is that it developed out of the answer given to a knock on the door of a pioneer cabin. The man of the house called out "Who's here" (or hyer)—and thereafter became known as a "Hoosier."

Probably the Hoosier's most sentimental attachment is to the Wabash. In every Hoosier heart the moonlight is still gleaming on the river, the new-mown hay lies along its banks in all its nostalgic splendor, and innumerable Hoosier Huck Finns still fish from under the sycamores.

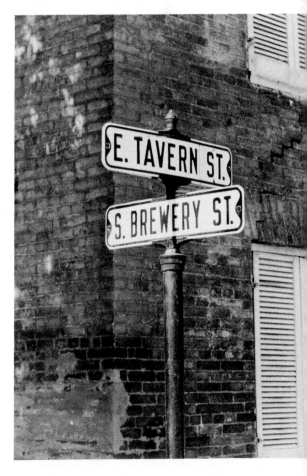

INDEX

We wish to thank those people who extended Hoosier hospitality on our trips through southern Indiana. Some 8,000 miles of road and 170 rolls of film ticked through the speedometer and the cameras. The photographs were made with Leica cameras—two M3 models and an M1 with Visoflex II housing. Lenses: 28mm, 35mm, 50mm, 90mm, 200mm, 400mm. Film: Tri-X rated at ASA 500.

Hartley and Jean Alley
Bloomington, Indiana
April, 1965

Photograph by Robert Talbot, Jr.

SOUTHERN INDIANA

Photographed by Hartley Alley

TEXT BY JEAN ALLEY

A TREAT for the eye, this exciting photographic treasury captures the heart of the cities, rural communities, unforgettable scenery, and colorful historic places of southern Indiana's rolling countryside. Nearly two hundred black-and-white prints portray Hoosiers at work and at play in an area which on the one hand boasts two-hundred-year-old buildings and preserves the homespun traditions of the early pioneer and riverboat days, and on the other hand offers the sophisticated cultural atmosphere of one of America's great universities, the brisk activity of modern industries, and some of the most distinguished avant-garde architecture of the twentieth century.

Magnificent photographic impressions highlight such historic sites and objects as the Indiana Territorial Capitol at Vincennes, where George Rogers Clark in 1779 won the entire Northwest for the colonies; Spencer County, where Lincoln spent his boyhood; the roofless church at New Harmony, the unique utopian community established by the Rappites in the early nineteenth century and setting of the significant educational and social experiments later conducted by the Owenites; the wooded hills of Brown County, famed for its undefiled natural

splendor—and its artists' colony. Also included are delightful photographs of Nashville's country stores, antique shops, and blacksmith shops; New Albany, whose flourishing riverboat industry produced the legendary steamboat, the *Robert E. Lee,* one hundred years ago; the Lanier Mansion at Madison, site of the magnificent collection of antebellum architecture designed by Francis Costigan; and, of course, southern Indiana's traditional industry—the limestone quarries.

HARTLEY and JEAN ALLEY, pictured above with their camper—custom designed and manufactured for their photographic expeditions by a firm in Vevay—are the authors of the popular full-length picture book *A Gentleman from Indiana Looks at Marblehead.* Mr. Alley has worked on many assignments for *Time, Life, Farm Journal, Saturday Evening Post,* and other national magazines. Mrs. Alley, who also designed SOUTHERN INDIANA, was a commercial artist before she turned to writing as a career. Residents of Bloomington, Indiana, the authors have for years explored every nook and cranny of the state's southern region, which they recreate so stunningly in this book.

$2.95

Also available in a clothbound edition at $5.00

INDIANA UNIVERSITY PRESS · BLOOMINGTON